The Wild Horses of Corolla

A Story Book YOU Can Color!

Linda Whittington Hurst

Wild Pony Press
Lake Charles, LA 70605
E-mail: linda@lindawhurst.com

ISBN-13: 978-1545505038
ISBN-10: 1545505039
Second Edition

The Story of the Wild Horses of Corolla

Long ago, there were no horses on the islands known today as the Outer Banks of North Carolina. Everyone knows that in 1492, when Columbus first discovered the West Indies, the entire world changed. The New World would be the answer to the problems of the Old World. Gold was discovered, making the New World even more important.

In 1584, Sir Walter Raleigh financed the first English colony in the New World. This colony was located on one of the barrier islands that hug the mainland of North America in what is now North Carolina.

This new colony was not destined to be successful. Out of supplies and desperate, the colonists begged the captain of the first English ship that passed by for passage back to England. Sir Frances Drake, the famous explorer and privateer, agreed to take them provided they left their animals behind. The colonists had purchased some mustangs from the Spanish. The colonists did not know whether these horses could survive the harsh climate and terrible storms that troubled their island home, but they had no choice. They turned their horses and cattle loose to live or die on their own.

Alone and desperate, the horses learned to take care of themselves. They ate the sea oats and salt grasses that grew on their sandy island. Fresh water was available and soon the herd grew. Life was hard, but they were tough.

At first, there were no humans living on these islands. Every now and then, a small band of Native Americans would come to hunt game, but most of the time the horses were left to survive on their own.

Soon, however, pirates discovered these islands and began to use them to hide their stolen treasure from the British ships. Blackbeard was the most famous of these pirates. Today, at dusk, you can sometimes see lights along the coastline. Rumor has it that these lights come from the ghosts of pirates who are returning to dig up their gold!

During the Revolutionary War, a small family lived near what is now Corolla, in a tiny house near the ocean. They made their living rescuing sailors who somehow survived the many shipwrecks that happened just off shore in this area now called "the Graveyard of the Atlantic". One day, a teenager named Betsy Dowdy overheard a spy say that the British were going to capture the American army at Great Bridge in Virginia, just north of Corolla. In desperation, Betsy jumped astride her formerly wild Corolla mustang. She and her horse swam across the wide Currituck Sound. Then she braved the darkness and dangers of the Great Dismal Swamp to warn the Americans. Her daring ride saved the day. The British were the ones who were surprised at Great Bridge!

Today, the wild Colonial Spanish Mustangs, sometimes called "Bankers", still roam the Outer Banks near the village of Corolla. However, their very existence is in danger due to the development of beach houses and the flood of visitors to this beautiful island coast. To learn more about these magnificent animals and how you can help save them from extinction please contact the Corolla Wild Horse Fund. Here is their website: www.corollawildhorses.com

Name: _____

The Corolla Wild Horse Fund is a non-profit organization whose goal is to save these wild horses. They have given all the horses in the herd a name, usually when they are foals. Color these two foals and then give them a name of your own.

Name: _____

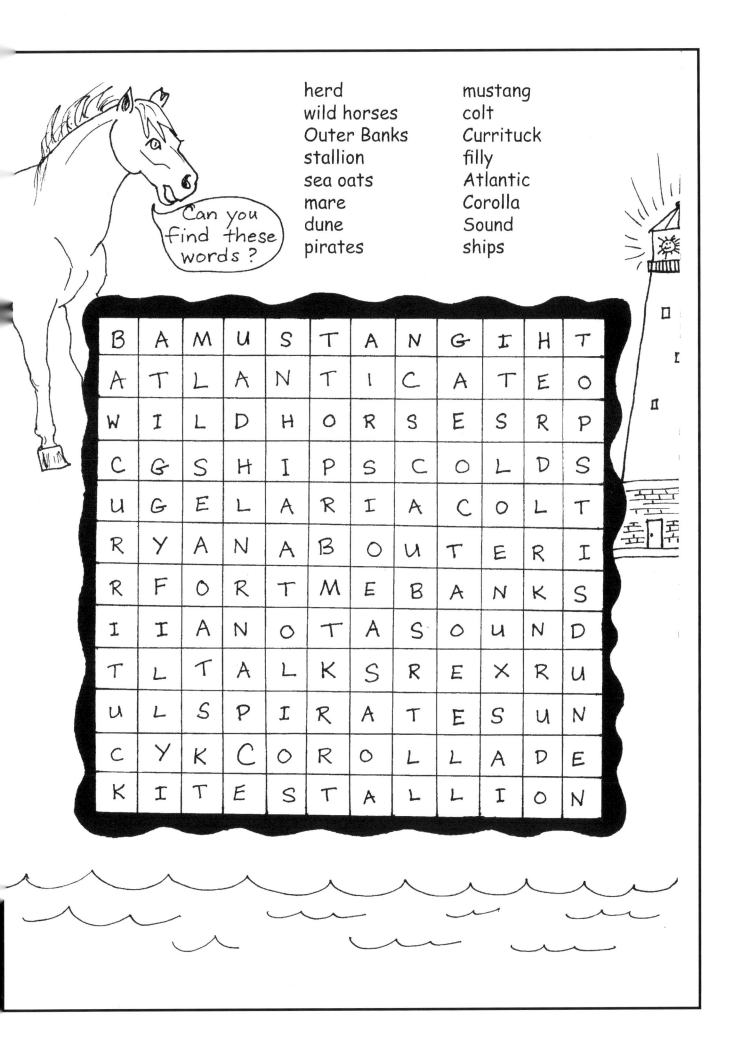

Can you find these words?

herd
wild horses
Outer Banks
stallion
sea oats
mare
dune
pirates

mustang
colt
Currituck
filly
Atlantic
Corolla
Sound
ships

B	A	M	U	S	T	A	N	G	I	H	T
A	T	L	A	N	T	I	C	A	T	E	O
W	I	L	D	H	O	R	S	E	S	R	P
C	G	S	H	I	P	S	C	O	L	D	S
U	G	E	L	A	R	I	A	C	O	L	T
R	Y	A	N	A	B	O	U	T	E	R	I
R	F	O	R	T	M	E	B	A	N	K	S
I	I	A	N	O	T	A	S	O	U	N	D
T	L	T	A	L	K	S	R	E	X	R	U
U	L	S	P	I	R	A	T	E	S	U	N
C	Y	K	C	O	R	O	L	L	A	D	E
K	I	T	E	S	T	A	L	L	I	O	N

Sir Walter Raleigh is responsible for the English colonists settling on the island of Manteo in the Outer Banks.

When the settlers realized that they could not support themselves at their settlement on the Outer Banks, they hitched a ride back to England with the first English ship that stopped for a visit. **Sir Francis Drake**, captain of the ship, agreed to take the settlers, but not their horses.

Pirates loved to hide their ships and their treasures on the islands now known as the Outer Banks. The most famous of these pirates was **Blackbeard**.

Blackbeard the pirate loved to hide treasure on the Outer Banks.

HALLOWEEN

Phantom ships are said to sail across the horizon on dark, foggy nights. On Halloween, locals sometimes entertain each other with eerie ghost stories.

The wild horses can often be seen
roaming along the beaches and cooling
off in the surf.

Visitors are warned to stay at least 50 feet away from the horses. Although they look tame, these animals are really wild and can be dangerous.

The wild horses are curious and are often attracted to the food and toys brought to the beach by vacationers. Sadly, because they are not used to eating foods like carrots and apples, feeding them can cause the horses to get sick and die.

avage storms like hurricanes are common during the spring,
ummer, and fall. Visitors and locals alike leave the island
nd head for the safety of the mainland with its higher
ound. But the horses must stay. They have learned how to
uddle together behind the safety of the tall sand dunes and
rub oaks during these treacherous storms.

The **Currituck Lighthouse** was once important for warning ships of the dangerous shoals near the island. Today, with modern technology, lighthouses are obsolete. The Currituck Lighthouse is now open for visitors to climb to the top and get a birds' eye view of the island.

Highway 12 is the main road that runs from Cape Hatteras in the south all the way to Corolla in the north. There are plans to extend this two-lane highway from Corolla to the state of Virginia. The main problem is that some people drive too fast on this highway. Unfortunately, each year wild horses are hit and killed by speeding cars.

Draw your own wild Corolla horse here!

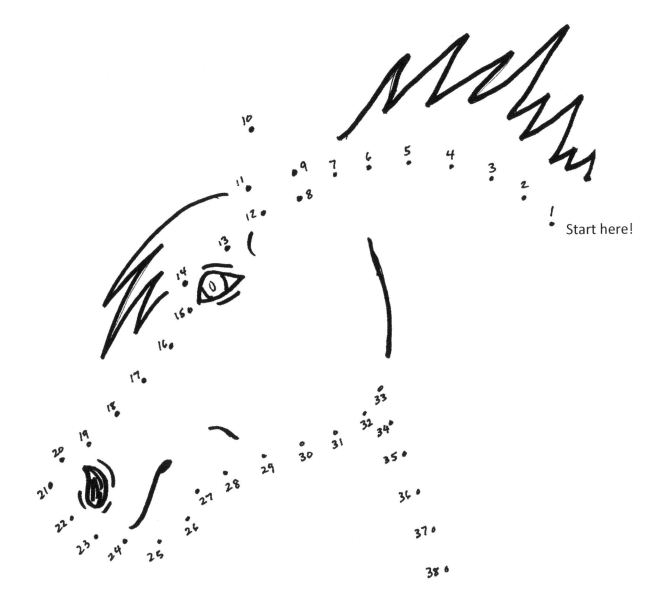

Start here!

Connect-the-Dots!

Start with number 1 and draw a line to each
consecutive number until you reach number
45. Now you have a picture to color!

Wild horses live together in small bands called "harems". Each harem has one stallion. During mating season, stallions fight over mares. Young stallions are driven away from the band and often live together in "bachelor" bands. In the spring, young stallions often challenge the older stallions for ownership of the harems.

During the heat of the summer, horses often cool off
in the waters along the shore of the Atlantic Ocean.

Mares and their colts can often be seen along the shoreline. Visitors are cautioned to keep at least 50 feet away from the wild horses. Mares are very protective of their babies and can be vicious if they feel endangered.

When they follow the rules vacationers can
enjoy both the beach and the wild horses.

Tradewind is a rescued Corolla wild stallion who foundered (became very ill) because he ate food his digestive system couldn't handle. When a horse founders, he becomes lame and cannot walk. Since a horse's only defense from predators is to run, if a wild horse becomes lame and cannot walk, he usually dies. To save Tradewind's life, he was captured and went to live at Mill Swamp Indian Horses farm. He not only recuperated (got well), this little stallion went on to win the **2011 National Pleasure Trail Horse of the Year Award**! In 2014, Karen McAlpin rode Tradewind in the World Horse Expo. For more information, check out this blogsite: https://msindianhorses.blogspot.com/2014/01/tradewind-at-world-horse-exposition.html?m=0

Manteo is one of the Corolla foundation stallions at Mill Creek Indian Horses. His offspring will help prevent the Colonial Spanish Mustang breed from becoming extinct.

Mill Swamp Indian Horses is a program of **Gwaltney Frontier Farm, Inc.**, a nonprofit breed conservation program. The program works to prevent the extinction of the wild horses known as Colonial Spanish Mustan, like the ones at Corolla. For more information, check out their website: www.millswampindianhorses.com

Naiche is a Chincoteague pony used in trail riding at Mill Creek Indian Horses. Chincoteague ponies come from the island of Assateague, one of the barrier islands along the Virginia-Maryland coastline.

Red Feather

Red Feather was a wild Corolla stallion who became famous because of his many adventures. He loved to steal apples from the local grocery store and ate trash out of the locals garbage cans. Worse, he would swim around the barrier fence to escape his island home and travel north to Virginia. On one such adventure with his entire harem, a colt was hit by a car. Because of this, both Red Feather and the colt had to be removed from the wild and placed at the rescue farm. Mr. Steve Edwards trained Red Feather well and he became a trail horse. Still, Red Feather was known for his occasional wild outbursts. This feisty mustang never forgot his wild heritage. His colts can be seen at the Gwaltney Frontier Farm. You can read all about this special horse in two books by author, Linda Hurst, entitled: ***The Adventures of Red Feather: Wild Horse of Corolla***, and ***Red Feather Goes to School.***

Red Feather was one of the wild Corolla horses that had to be removed to a rescue farm. Pictured above are Red Feather and his trainer, **Steve Edwards**. Today, Steve is dedicated to the rescue and preservation of the Colonial Spanish Mustangs, including horses from Corolla, Shackleford and other barrier islands along the shores of the Atlantic. Steve invites you to visit his website to learn more about this important project (see below).

Other books about the wild horses of Corolla by Linda Whittington Hurst:

- ***The Adventures of Red Feather: Wild Horse of Corolla*** (hard back - picture book)
- ***Red Feather Goes to School*** (hard back - picture book)
- ***Saving Wild Thunder*** (paperback - middle grade novel)
- ***Wild and Free*** (paperback - picture book)
- ***Summer of the Wild Horses*** (paperback - chapter book)
- ***My Chincoteague Pony Coloring Book*** - paperback

    Books are available on Amazon.com, www.lindawhurst.com, the bookstore at the Corolla Wild Horse Fund (www.corollawildhorses.com), Corolla, NC, Mill Swamp Indian Horses (www.millswampindianhorses.com), and Sundial Books, Chincoteague Island.

Linda Whittington Hurst

Made in the USA
Columbia, SC
23 May 2023

1674363OR00020